A ROOKIE BIOGRAPHY

EMILY DICKINSON

American Poet

By Carol Greene

CHILDRENS PRESS®
CHICAGO

Emily Dickinson (1830-1886)

Library of Congress Cataloging-in-Publication Data

Greene, Carol.
    Emily Dickinson : American poet / by Carol Greene.
       p.   cm.
    ISBN 0-516-04263-7
    1. Dickinson, Emily, 1830-1886—Biography—Juvenile literature.
    2. Women poets, American—19th century—Biography—Juvenile
    literature. [1. Dickinson, Emily, 1830-1886. 2. Poets, American.
    3. Women—Biography.] I. Greene, Carol. Rookie biography. II. Title.
    PS1541.Z5G69   1994
    811′.4—dc20
    [B]   94-11167
                                                             CIP
                                                              AC

Emily Dickinson
was a real person.
She was born in 1830.
She died in 1886.
Emily lived a quiet life
and wrote great poems.
This is her story.

TABLE OF CONTENTS

Emily was born in this home (above) in Amherst, Massachusetts.
Below is a view of Amherst as it looked in the 1830s.

Chapter 1

Emily Is Emily

"Where *is* Emily?"

Emily Dickinson
could hear her family
looking for her.
But she did not move
or make a sound.

"Everyone in the house
must be ready
for Sunday school
in ten minutes,"
Father had said.

But Emily did not want
to go to Sunday school.
So she sat in the
opening to the cellar.

6

Father had said,
"Everyone *in* the house."
But Emily was not
in the house.
So, she thought, she
did not have to obey.

And the family went
to Sunday school
without her.

This painting shows Emily (left), her brother Austin (center), and her sister Lavinia (Vinnie).

Emily's brother, Austin,
and her sister, Vinnie,
were good children.
Emily was good too—
most of the time.

But Emily had
her own ideas.
Sometimes she just knew
what was right for her
and she did it.

"Don't go into the woods,"
said the grown-ups.
"Goblins might get you.
A snake might bite you.
You might be poisoned
by a flower."

Emily walked in the beautiful woods near her home.

"But I need to go into the woods,"
thought Emily.
And into the woods she went.

There, she wrote later,
she met only angels.
And they were more shy of her
than she was of them.

The angels Emily met
were probably birds,
flowers, and animals.
The little things of nature
were always dear to her.

Emily loved the birds and wildflowers she saw in the woods.

Emily's father
was tall and
stern and wise.
People in Amherst,
Massachusetts,
thought he was
a fine man. They
called him Squire.

Emily's father,
Edward Dickinson

Emily thought her father
was a fine man too.
But sometimes,
just sometimes,
she knew what was
right for Emily.

And Emily had
to be Emily.

Emily Dickinson
as a young girl

Emily went to school at Amherst Academy on Amity Street in Amherst.

Chapter 2

Growing and Learning

When Emily was nine,
she started school at
the Amherst Academy.
It was a very good school
and Emily felt proud
to be part of it.

She studied Latin,
geology, botany,
and philosophy.
"How large they sound,
don't they?" she wrote
to a friend.

Emily also had
fun at school.
She and four other girls
formed their own club.
They talked a lot
about teachers and boys.

But sometimes Emily
and her friends were sad.
In those days,
people could die
of simple diseases.
Many children died too.

Emily often thought about death and God. She wasn't really sure what she believed. But she wanted to figure it out herself.

When Emily was 16, her father sent her to Mount Holyoke, a girls' school not too far from Amherst.

Emily Dickinson at about 16 years old

Mount Holyoke as it looked about 1845

At first, Emily liked
that school too.
But then some things
began to bother her.

The teachers wanted
all the girls
to believe in God
exactly as they did.

18

In this picture cut out of black paper, the Dickinson
family is shown visiting Emily at Mount Holyoke.

Emily couldn't do that.
She had to find
her own way to believe.
Emily had to be Emily.

Emily didn't make
as many good friends
as she had before either.
That was hard.

At last Emily caught
a very bad cold.
Her cough wouldn't go away.
So her father sent Austin
to bring her home.

And soon Emily felt better.
Home, she learned, was
the best place for her.
At home she could be Emily.

The Dickinson house in Amherst

Chapter 3

At Home

Emily had plenty
to do at home.
She liked to bake
and work in the garden.

Emily cheered up
her mother too.
Her mother
was often sick.
And Emily fussed
over her stern,
stuffy father.

Emily Dickinson's mother

Austin Dickinson in 1850

Vinnie Dickinson in 1852

But Emily's favorite people
were Austin and Vinnie,
her brother and sister.
When they went away to
school, Emily missed them.
But they both came back.

Austin married Sue,
one of Emily's friends.
Emily's father gave
Austin and Sue a house
next door to his.

Austin Dickinson
married Susan Gilbert,
Emily's friend (below).
Austin and Susan lived
in this house (left)
next door to Emily.

For a while, Vinnie was
also going to get married.
But she didn't.
She stayed home too.

Emily spent a lot of time
writing letters to her friends.
She also wrote poems,
but not very many.

Still, she was learning
how to look at things
the way a poet does.

Vinnie Dickinson and a friend

Emily wrote about the simple things of nature, such as sunsets, flowers, and small creatures.

She looked at birds, at flowers in spring, at purple sunsets, and at a little snake slipping through the grass.

Someday soon, Emily
would turn her thoughts
about these things into poems.

But first, something sad
happened to Emily.
She fell in love
with the wrong man.

Charles Wadsworth
already had a wife.

He could be Emily's friend,
but nothing more.

That was hard for Emily.
But somehow it helped
her start writing poems.
And soon those poems
were the most important
thing in her life.

Charles
Wadsworth

Chapter 4

The Poems

"Bring me the sunset in a cup,"
wrote Emily.

And

"I'm Nobody! Who are you?
Are you—Nobody—Too?"

And

"Two Butterflies went out at Noon—
And waltzed upon a Farm—"

Thomas Higginson

After a while, Emily sent
a few of her poems to
Thomas Higginson.
He was an important writer.

Thomas Higginson
met with his
publisher at
The Old Corner
Book-Store in Boston,
Massachusetts.

Mr. Higginson thought
Emily's poems were interesting.
But he didn't think
most people would like them.
They were too different.

Soon Emily decided that
only special people,
like her family and friends,
would read her poems
while she was alive.

But that didn't stop
Emily from writing them.
In just one year,
she wrote 366 poems.
By the end of her life,
she had written 1,775.

Emily worked so hard
at her poems that
her eyes began to hurt.
She had to go to Boston
to have them treated.
Vinnie went with her.

A street in Boston in the 1860s

But still Emily wrote.
At last the little snake
found his way into a poem.

"A narrow fellow in the Grass
Occasionally rides—"

One poem was a letter
from a fly to a bee.

"Bee! I'm expecting you!"

At left is a portrait of Emily. Above is a poem by Emily, written on the flap of an envelope and sent to "Sister Sue."

Emily copied her poems
into little books she made.
Her writing looked like
the footprints of birds.
Then she put the books
into a large box.

Maybe someday someone
would want to read them.

Chapter 5

Emily the Poet

As the years passed,
Emily saw fewer people
outside her family.
She wore white dresses
and mostly stayed at home.

But Emily always liked
to see little children.
She played games with them
and made them presents.
She kept a jar full of
cookies for them too.

Emily's nephew Gilbert (Gib) Dickinson

As Emily grew older,
people in her family
began to die.
Her father died first,
then her mother.
That was hard.

But it was even harder
when her nephew Gib died.
He was only eight years old.

Otis Lord

But as Emily grew older,
a good thing happened too.
She fell in love with
a man named Otis Lord
and he fell in love with her.

They didn't get married,
but they still made
each other happy.

When Otis Lord died,
Emily seemed to give up.
She lived two more years,
but she was sick
most of the time.

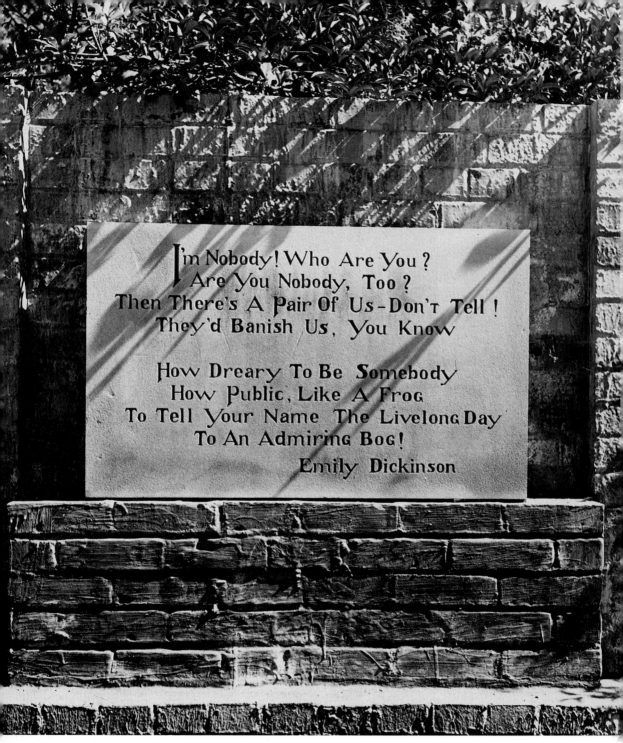

I'm Nobody! Who Are You?
Are You Nobody, Too?
Then There's A Pair Of Us — Don't Tell!
They'd Banish Us, You Know

How Dreary To Be Somebody
How Public, Like A Frog
To Tell Your Name The Livelong Day
To An Admiring Bog!

Emily Dickinson

One of Emily's most famous poems is carved on this stone.

Vinnie took good care of her,
but on May 15, 1886,
Emily Dickinson died.

Her life had been
a quiet one.
Many people would say
that nothing important
ever happened to Emily.

But in her poems,
Emily flew with birds
and danced with butterflies.
She leaned against the sun,
talked with God, and
found her own way to believe.

Roses on a stone wall

In her poems,
Emily was Emily.
And the time came
when people everywhere
were glad that she was.

Important Dates

1830   December 10—Born in Amherst, Massachusetts, to Emily and Edward Dickinson

1840   Began studies at Amherst Academy

1846   Began studies at Mount Holyoke Female Seminary

1848   Returned home to stay

1862   First wrote Thomas Higginson about her poems

1864-1865   Trips to Boston for eye treatment

1874   Father died

1882   Mother died

1883   Nephew Gilbert (Gib) Dickinson died

1884   Otis Lord died

1886   May 15—Died in Amherst, Massachusetts

INDEX

Page numbers in boldface type indicate illustrations.

PHOTO CREDITS

ABOUT THE AUTHOR

Carol Greene has degrees in English literature and musicology. She has worked in international exchange programs, as an editor, and as a teacher of writing. She now lives in Webster Groves, Missouri, and writes full-time. She has published more than 100 books, including those in the Childrens Press Rookie Biographies series.